The Yorkshire Dales Trig-Baggers Logbook

Trig points, or trigonometrical stations to give them their proper name, are a common sight and much-loved feature of Britain's hills. Constructed between 1936-1962 as part of the Ordnance Survey's Retriangulation of Great Britain, this log book is your ideal hiking companion as you bag them all in the Yorkshire Dales.

This log book contains over 100 trig points to be found in the Yorkshire Dales National Park, the Nidderdale Area of Outstanding Natural Beauty and the Rombalds Moor to Skipton Moor area of lower Wharfedale and Airedale – as well as a couple which sit just outside of the national park bound

CW01496816

each page
with your phone
to open a map of the
trig point

TOP TIP:
You can zoom in and out on the map on your phone by pressing the [+] and [-] buttons. Take screenhots in case you are out of mobile data on the hills!

Using the book is easy, use the map page to plan your next adventure and scan the QR code using your smartphone on the page of the trig you are planning on bagging to open a map of the trig point. We have included a few facts on each trig, as well as height info, date built and OS grid reference for you to enter into your GPS.

 Make sure when you have bagged your trig points, tick them off on the contents page and fill in the tick on your log page after you have filled in your adventure details!

Some of the trig points in this book have sadly been destroyed over the years - expanding quaries have unfortunately swallowed a few of them up. We have still included them as the sites they were located at are still worth a visit.
Have fun planning your hikes & enjoy the Yorkshire Dales & beyond!

1 Addlebrough	38 Harper Hill	75 Overgate Croft Farm
2 Askwith Moor	39 Hartwith	76 Park Fell
3 Aye Gill Pike	40 Haw Crag	77 Parsons Pulpit
4 Beamsley Beacon	41 Haw Pike	78 Pen-Y-Ghent
5 Bishopside Brae	42 Heyshaw Moor	79 Penhill
6 Blea Moor	43 High Seat	80 Powson Knott
7 Booze Moor	44 Holme Knott	81 Rain Stang Hill
8 Brimham Rocks	45 Hoove Faggergill	82 Ravensworth Fell
9 Brownthwaite	46 Horse Head	83 Rivock Edge
10 Buckden Pike	47 Hunter Bark	84 Rombalds Moor
11 Caley Deer Park	48 Ingleborough	85 Rye Loaf
12 Calf Top	49 Kelleth Rigg	86 Sail Hill
13 Calton	50 Kettlestang Hill	87 Sandy Hill
14 Camp Hill	51 Kex Gill Moor	88 Scrafton
15 Carr Top	52 Kilnsey Moor	89 Sharpah
16 Cave Hill	53 Knowe Fell	90 Simons Seat
17 Citron Seat	54 Langcliffe	91 Smearsett Scar
18 Collinsons Hill	55 Langerton Hill	92 Stone Beds
19 Colsterdale Moor	56 Lanshaw Farm	93 Stonesdale Moor
20 Conistone Moor	57 Lindley Moor	94 Sulber
21 Copperthwaite Moor	58 Ling Park	95 Swinden
22 Cosh Outside	59 Little Whernside	96 Telfit Moor
23 Cow Close Fell	60 Low Green Field Lings	97 The Calf
24 Crag Hill	61 Mark Hill	98 The Chevin
25 Crook Rise Crag Top	62 Maulds Meaburn Moor	99 The Fleak
26 Delph Farm	63 Meugher	100 The Weets
27 Dodd Fell	64 Middleham Low Moor	101 Thorpe Fell
28 East Baugh Fell	65 Middlesmoor Pasture	102 Tow Scar
29 Firth Fell	66 Middleton	103 Vicars Allotment
30 Gragareth Fell	67 Moughton	104 Water Crag
31 Great Knoutberry Hill	68 Nettle Hill	105 Whaw Moor
32 Great Shunner Fell	69 New Pasture Edge	106 Whit Fell
33 Great Whernside	70 Newsham Moor	107 Wild Boar Fell
34 Green Bell	71 Newton Moor	108 Winder Hill
35 Greenhow Moor	72 Nine Standards Rigg	109 Windy Hill
36 Grey Grit	73 North Nab	110 Witton Fell
37 Halton Height	74 Ouster Bank	111 Yockenthwaite Moor

The Yorkshire Dales

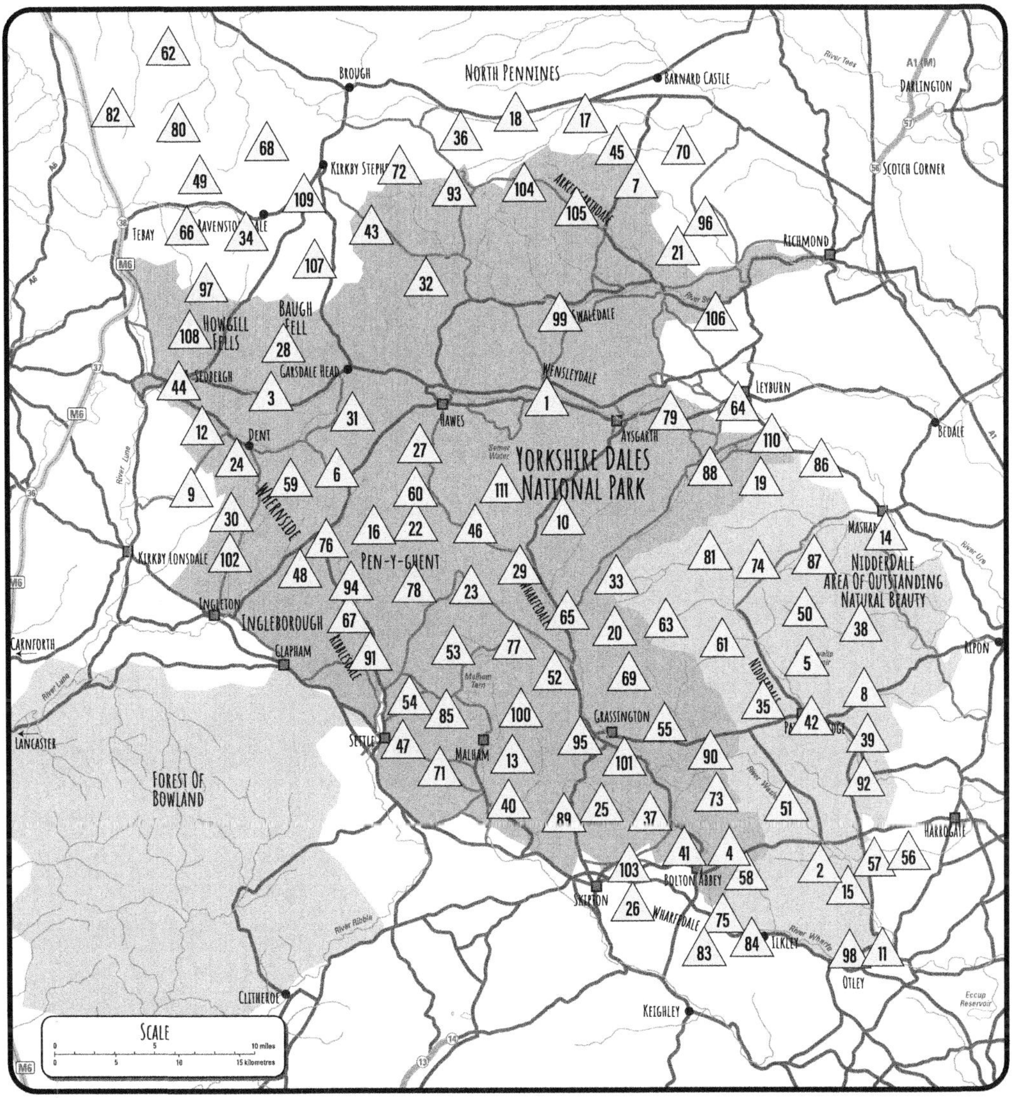

Map labels and numbered markers:

BROUGH · NORTH PENNINES · BARNARD CASTLE · River Tees · A1(M) · DARLINGTON · SCOTCH CORNER · RICHMOND · BEDALE · LEYBURN · MASHAM · RIPON · HARROGATE · KEIGHLEY · OTLEY · Eccup Reservoir · LANCASTER · CARNFORTH · CLITHEROE · SKIPTON · SETTLE · CLAPHAM · INGLETON · KIRKBY LONSDALE · DENT · SEDBERGH · TEBAY · KIRKBY STEPHEN · RAVENSTONEDALE · GARSDALE HEAD · HAWES · AYSGARTH · GRASSINGTON · MALHAM · BOLTON ABBEY · ILKLEY

Yorkshire Dales National Park · Forest Of Bowland · Nidderdale Area Of Outstanding Natural Beauty · Howgill Fells · Baugh Fell · Wensleydale · Swaledale · Arkengarthdale · Mallerstang · Pen-y-ghent · Ingleborough · Wharfedale · Nidderdale · Malham Tarn · Semer Water

Numbered triangle markers: 62, 82, 80, 68, 49, 18, 36, 17, 45, 70, 7, 96, 21, 106, 72, 93, 104, 105, 109, 43, 32, 99, 107, 97, 28, 108, 44, 3, 31, 1, 79, 64, 110, 88, 19, 86, 12, 24, 9, 30, 102, 59, 6, 27, 60, 46, 10, 111, 16, 22, 48, 76, 94, 78, 23, 29, 33, 81, 74, 87, 14, 67, 91, 53, 77, 65, 20, 63, 61, 50, 38, 5, 8, 54, 85, 100, 52, 69, 55, 35, 42, 39, 92, 47, 71, 13, 95, 101, 90, 73, 51, 40, 89, 25, 37, 41, 4, 58, 2, 57, 56, 15, 103, 26, 75, 84, 98, 11, 83

SCALE

0 — 5 — 10 miles
0 — 5 — 10 — 15 kilometres

Yorkshire Dales Map:

Trig Finder - In Alphabetical Order

Notes

Trig Finder - In Height Ascending Order

Trig Finder - In County Order

Equipment Checklist

Addlebrough

Height (m): 477m · Date Built: 20th August 1953 · County: North Yorkshire
Nearest Town: Richmond · OS Grid Reference: SD946881

The trig point was removed in about 2001 by the Yorkshire Dales National Park and the National Trust who own Addlebrough. It was done to protect the nearby cup & ring marked rock from hordes of hikers they were expecting when open access came into effect.

Date	Parking ★★★★★	Map Ref: /1\

Ascent Start Time	Trig Time

Descent Start Time	Finish Time

Ascent Duration	Descent Duration	Total Time

Total Distance Covered	No. Of Steps

Companions

Weather

Enjoyment ○○○○○○○○○○
Views ○○○○○○○○○○
Difficulty ○○○○○○○○○○

Highlights

Notes

Askwith Moor

Height (m): 301m · Date Built: 16th November 1953 · County: North Yorkshire
Nearest Town: Otley · OS Grid Reference: SE171510

A fairly easy trig point to reach, approx. a quarter mile from the road situated on a good track. A good panorama surrounded by heather with views over the Washburn/lower Wharfdale area.

Date	Parking ★ ★ ★ ★ ★	Map Ref: 2

Ascent Start Time	Trig Time

Descent Start Time	Finish Time

Ascent Duration	Descent Duration	Total Time

Total Distance Covered	No. Of Steps

Companions

Weather

Enjoyment ○ ○ ○ ○ ○ ○ ○ ○ ○ ○
Views ○ ○ ○ ○ ○ ○ ○ ○ ○ ○
Difficulty ○ ○ ○ ○ ○ ○ ○ ○ ○ ○

Highlights

Notes

Aye Gill Pike

Height (m): 557m · Date Built: 1st September 1949 · County: Cumbria
Nearest Town: Kendal · OS Grid Reference: SD720886
The view is dominated by Great Coum and Whernside to the south and Baugh Fell to the north. Situated next to a broken wall which almost runs the full length of Rise Hill.

Date	Parking ★★★★★	Map Ref: /3\

Ascent Start Time		Trig Time
Descent Start Time		Finish Time

Ascent Duration	Descent Duration	Total Time

Total Distance Covered		No. Of Steps

Companions

Weather

Enjoyment	○	○	○	○	○	○	○	○	○	○
Views	○	○	○	○	○	○	○	○	○	○
Difficulty	○	○	○	○	○	○	○	○	○	○

Highlights

Notes

Beamsley Beacon

Height (m): 393m · Date Built: 30th April 1949 · County: North Yorkshire
Nearest Town: Ilkley · OS Grid Reference: SE098524

Situated about a quarter of a mile south-west of the highest point of the fell which is situated on The Old Pike. The views are superb, especially to the north up the valley of Wharfedale, South include Rombald's Moor beyond the South Pennines.

Date	Parking ★★★★★	Map Ref: 4

Ascent Start Time		Trig Time	

Descent Start Time		Finish Time	

Ascent Duration	Descent Duration	Total Time

Total Distance Covered	No. Of Steps

Companions

Weather

Enjoyment	○ ○ ○ ○ ○ ○ ○ ○ ○ ○
Views	○ ○ ○ ○ ○ ○ ○ ○ ○ ○
Difficulty	○ ○ ○ ○ ○ ○ ○ ○ ○ ○

Highlights

Notes

Bishopside Brae

Height (m): 351m · Date Built: 29th October 1953 · County: North Yorkshire
Nearest Town: Ripon · OS Grid Reference: SE159673

Built on a small mound surrounded by grass and a few rocks, Situated towards the top end of a heathery pasture - easily reached via a gate on Wath Lane.

Date	Parking ★★★★★	Map Ref: 5

Ascent Start Time	Trig Time

Descent Start Time	Finish Time

Ascent Duration	Descent Duration	Total Time

Total Distance Covered	No. Of Steps

Companions

Weather

Enjoyment	○ ○ ○ ○ ○ ○ ○ ○ ○ ○
Views	○ ○ ○ ○ ○ ○ ○ ○ ○ ○
Difficulty	○ ○ ○ ○ ○ ○ ○ ○ ○ ○

Highlights

Notes

Blea Moor

Height (m): 536m · Date Built: 3rd September 1949 · County: North Yorkshire
Nearest Town: Kendal · OS Grid Reference: SD772825
The trig point can be reached from the footpath to the north which follows the line of the Bleamoor Tunnel. The path can be accessed
from Ribblehead or from Dent Head

Date	Parking ★ ★ ★ ★ ★	Map Ref: △ 6

Ascent Start Time	Trig Time

Descent Start Time	Finish Time

Ascent Duration	Descent Duration	Total Time

Total Distance Covered	No. Of Steps

Companions

Weather

Enjoyment ○ ○ ○ ○ ○ ○ ○ ○ ○ ○

Views ○ ○ ○ ○ ○ ○ ○ ○ ○ ○

Difficulty ○ ○ ○ ○ ○ ○ ○ ○ ○ ○

Highlights

Notes

Booze Moor

Height (m): 522m · Date Built: Not known · County: North Yorkshire
Nearest Town: Richmond · OS Grid Reference: NZ017049

A fairly rough and pathless walk to the trig point which is to the south of the Stang road between Arkengarthdale and Teesdale. The easiest approach is by the shooting track that passes within a third of a mile to the south-east of the trig point itself.

Date	Parking ★★★★★	Map Ref: /7\
Ascent Start Time		Trig Time
Descent Start Time		Finish Time
Ascent Duration	Descent Duration	Total Time
Total Distance Covered		No. Of Steps
Companions		

Weather

Enjoyment ○○○○○○○○○○
Views ○○○○○○○○○○
Difficulty ○○○○○○○○○○

Highlights

Notes

Brimham Rocks

Height (m): 301m · Date Built: 31st March 1954 · County: North Yorkshire
Nearest Town: Harrogate · OS Grid Reference: SE206650
The view from the Brimham Rocks trig point is impressive, especially to the south and south-east where it is virtually uninterrupted

Date	Parking ★ ★ ★ ★ ★	Map Ref: △ 8

Ascent Start Time	Trig Time

Descent Start Time	Finish Time

Ascent Duration	Descent Duration	Total Time

Total Distance Covered	No. Of Steps

Companions

Weather

Enjoyment ○ ○ ○ ○ ○ ○ ○ ○ ○ ○
Views   ○ ○ ○ ○ ○ ○ ○ ○ ○ ○
Difficulty ○ ○ ○ ○ ○ ○ ○ ○ ○ ○

Highlights

Notes

Brownthwaite

Height (m): 437m · Date Built: 1st May 1949 · County: Cumbria
Nearest Town: Carnforth · OS Grid Reference: SD650808

The view from the Brownthwaite trig point is largely dominated by the higher fells in the region such as Calf Top, Crag Hill, Great Coum & Gragareth. However the view to the south is quite extensive and includes the north Bowland fells.

Date	Parking ★★★★★★	Map Ref: /9\

Ascent Start Time	Trig Time
Descent Start Time	Finish Time

Ascent Duration	Descent Duration	Total Time

Total Distance Covered	No. Of Steps

Companions

Weather

Enjoyment	○	○	○	○	○	○	○	○	○	○
Views	○	○	○	○	○	○	○	○	○	○
Difficulty	○	○	○	○	○	○	○	○	○	○

Highlights

Notes

Buckden Pike

Height (m): 702m · Date Built: 16th July 1949 · County: North Yorkshire
Nearest Town: Richmond · OS Grid Reference: SD960787

If you're lucky enough to visit the top of Buckden Pike in good conditions then you will be able to enjoy an excellent view that includes the famous Yorkshire Three Peaks of Pen-y-ghent, Ingleborough and Whernside

Date	Parking ★ ★ ★ ★ ★	Map Ref: /10\
Ascent Start Time		Trig Time
Descent Start Time		Finish Time
Ascent Duration	Descent Duration	Total Time
Total Distance Covered		No. Of Steps
Companions		

Weather

Enjoyment ○ ○ ○ ○ ○ ○ ○ ○ ○ ○

Views ○ ○ ○ ○ ○ ○ ○ ○ ○ ○

Difficulty ○ ○ ○ ○ ○ ○ ○ ○ ○ ○

Highlights

Notes

Caley Deer Park

Height (m): 243m · Date Built: 6th October 1937 · County: West Yorkshire
Nearest Town: Otley · OS Grid Reference: SE224442

The trig point is very easy to reach, being only a ten minute walk on a track from a car park on East Chevin Road. Surrounded by woods, the view from this trig point is probably the most restricted of any of the trig points in Yorkshire!

Date	Parking ★★★★★★	Map Ref: 11

Ascent Start Time	Trig Time
Descent Start Time	Finish Time

Ascent Duration	Descent Duration	Total Time

Total Distance Covered	No. Of Steps

Companions

Weather

Enjoyment ○ ○ ○ ○ ○ ○ ○ ○ ○ ○

Views ○ ○ ○ ○ ○ ○ ○ ○ ○ ○

Difficulty ○ ○ ○ ○ ○ ○ ○ ○ ○ ○

Highlights

Notes

Calf Top

Height (m): 610m · Date Built: 1st July 1949 · County: Cumbria
Nearest Town: Kendal · OS Grid Reference: SD664856
On a clear day you can enjoy a superb panorama of the Dales, Howgill Fells, a long Lakeland skyline and the small hills around Arnside & Silverdale.

Date		Parking ★ ★ ★ ★ ★	Map Ref: /12\

Ascent Start Time		Trig Time	
Descent Start Time		Finish Time	

Ascent Duration	Descent Duration	Total Time

Total Distance Covered	No. Of Steps

Companions

Weather

Enjoyment	○ ○ ○ ○ ○ ○ ○ ○ ○ ○
Views	○ ○ ○ ○ ○ ○ ○ ○ ○ ○
Difficulty	○ ○ ○ ○ ○ ○ ○ ○ ○ ○

Highlights

Notes

Calton

Height (m): 275m · Date Built: 2nd June 1949 · County: North Yorkshire
Nearest Town: Barnoldswick · OS Grid Reference: SD917598
Situated just over half a mile from the village of Calton, on Calton Moor and was built in 1949. Nearby waterfalls make this a beautiful area to visit.

Date	Parking ★ ★ ★ ★ ★	Map Ref: 13
Ascent Start Time		Trig Time
Descent Start Time		Finish Time
Ascent Duration	Descent Duration	Total Time
Total Distance Covered		No. Of Steps
Companions		

Weather

Enjoyment	○	○	○	○	○	○	○	○	○ ○
Views	○	○	○	○	○	○	○	○	○ ○
Difficulty	○	○	○	○	○	○	○	○	○ ○

Highlights

Notes

Camp Hill

Height (m): 215m · Date Built: 4th July 1953 · County: North Yorkshire
Nearest Town: Ripon · OS Grid Reference: SE225774
Located next to a broken wall underneath a stand of trees and is fairly easy to locate from a nearby right of way. Views can be restricted, especially if the trees are in leaf.

Date	Parking ★ ★ ★ ★ ★	Map Ref: /14\

Ascent Start Time		Trig Time	
Descent Start Time		Finish Time	

Ascent Duration	Descent Duration	Total Time

Total Distance Covered	No. Of Steps

Companions

Weather

Enjoyment	○ ○ ○ ○ ○ ○ ○ ○ ○ ○
Views	○ ○ ○ ○ ○ ○ ○ ○ ○ ○
Difficulty	○ ○ ○ ○ ○ ○ ○ ○ ○ ○

Highlights

Notes

Carr Top

Height (m): 257m · Date Built: 13th November 1953 · County: North Yorkshire
Nearest Town: Otley · OS Grid Reference: SE193492

Located above a small abandoned quarry near Weston Moor Road between Blubberhouses and Otley. The views are good, particularly eastwards towards Lindley Moor and Great Almscliff Crag.

Date	Parking ☆☆☆☆☆	Map Ref: 15

Ascent Start Time	Trig Time

Descent Start Time	Finish Time

Ascent Duration	Descent Duration	Total Time

Total Distance Covered	No. Of Steps

Companions

Weather

Enjoyment ○○○○○○○○○○

Views ○○○○○○○○○○

Difficulty ○○○○○○○○○○

Highlights

Notes

Cave Hill

Height (m): 385m · Date Built: 9th September 1949 · County: North Yorkshire
Nearest Town: Barnoldswick · OS Grid Reference: SD803778
A fine viewpoint to see upper Ribblesdale. The panorama includes the likes of Simon Fell, Park Fell, Whernside, Cam Fell and Cosh Knott. Beautiful on a fine day.

Date	Parking ★ ★ ★ ★ ★	Map Ref: 16

Ascent Start Time	Trig Time

Descent Start Time	Finish Time

Ascent Duration	Descent Duration	Total Time

Total Distance Covered	No. Of Steps

Companions

Weather

Enjoyment ○ ○ ○ ○ ○ ○ ○ ○ ○ ○

Views ○ ○ ○ ○ ○ ○ ○ ○ ○ ○

Difficulty ○ ○ ○ ○ ○ ○ ○ ○ ○ ○

Highlights

Notes

Citron Seat

Height (m): 446m • Date Built: 14th September 1948 • County: Durham
Nearest Town: Barnard Castle • OS Grid Reference: NY977102

Citron Seat trig point is less than half a mile north of the national park boundary on a noticeable moorland bump on the summit of Gilmonby Moor.

Date	Parking ★★★★★★★	Map Ref: /17\

Ascent Start Time	Trig Time
Descent Start Time	Finish Time

Ascent Duration	Descent Duration	Total Time

Total Distance Covered	No. Of Steps

Companions

Weather

Enjoyment	○ ○ ○ ○ ○ ○ ○ ○ ○ ○
Views	○ ○ ○ ○ ○ ○ ○ ○ ○ ○
Difficulty	○ ○ ○ ○ ○ ○ ○ ○ ○ ○

Highlights

Notes

Collinsons Hill

Height (m): 435m · Date Built: 11th November 1947 · County: Durham
Nearest Town: Barnard Castle · OS Grid Reference: NY922104
Possibly one of the remotest and least visited of all the trig points, it is a long but surprisingly easy walk to reach, largely due to the good track that leaves the Pennine Way and crosses Bowes Moor.

Date	Parking ★ ★ ★ ★ ★	Map Ref: /18\
Ascent Start Time		Trig Time
Descent Start Time		Finish Time

Ascent Duration	Descent Duration	Total Time

Total Distance Covered	No. Of Steps

Companions

Weather

Enjoyment	○ ○ ○ ○ ○ ○ ○ ○ ○ ○
Views	○ ○ ○ ○ ○ ○ ○ ○ ○ ○
Difficulty	○ ○ ○ ○ ○ ○ ○ ○ ○ ○

Highlights

Notes

Colsterdale Moor

Height (m): 365m · Date Built: 24th September 1953 · County: North Yorkshire
Nearest Town: Richmond · OS Grid Reference: SE119815

Situated on the eastern flank of the moor of the same name above the valley of Colsterdale, views are restricted by higher ground to the west but are quite extensive to the east where there is a fairly uninterrupted view as far as the distant North York Moors.

Date	Parking ☆☆☆☆☆	Map Ref: /19\

Ascent Start Time	Trig Time

Descent Start Time	Finish Time

Ascent Duration	Descent Duration	Total Time

Total Distance Covered	No. Of Steps

Companions

Weather

Enjoyment ○○○○○○○○○○

Views ○○○○○○○○○○

Difficulty ○○○○○○○○○○

Highlights

Notes

Conistone Moor

Height (m): 513m · Date Built: 12th September 1949 · County: North Yorkshire
Nearest Town: Skipton · OS Grid Reference: SE001699

The trig point is situated on the edge of the moor of the same name at a spot called Capplestone Gate. It can be reached via an enjoyable climb via Gurling Trough, Conistone Dib & the old track known as the Conistone Turf Road.

Date	Parking ★ ★ ★ ★ ★	Map Ref: /20\

Ascent Start Time	Trig Time
Descent Start Time	Finish Time

Ascent Duration	Descent Duration	Total Time

Total Distance Covered	No. Of Steps

Companions

Weather

Enjoyment	○ ○ ○ ○ ○ ○ ○ ○ ○ ○
Views	○ ○ ○ ○ ○ ○ ○ ○ ○ ○
Difficulty	○ ○ ○ ○ ○ ○ ○ ○ ○ ○

Highlights

Notes

Copperthwaite Moor

Height (m): 430m · Date Built: 16th March 1948 · County: North Yorkshire
Nearest Town: Richmond · OS Grid Reference: SE057997

The Copperthwaite Moor trig point is located to the east of Fremington Edge and lies about 750ft outside the boundary of the national park.

Date	Parking ★★★★★★★	Map Ref: 21
Ascent Start Time		Trig Time
Descent Start Time		Finish Time
Ascent Duration	Descent Duration	Total Time
Total Distance Covered		No. Of Steps
Companions		

Weather

Enjoyment ○○○○○○○○○○

Views ○○○○○○○○○○

Difficulty ○○○○○○○○○○

Highlights

Notes

Cosh Outside

Height (m): 600m · Date Built: 8th October 1949 · County: North Yorkshire
Nearest Town: Barnoldswick · OS Grid Reference: SD836780
Cosh Outside trig point is located on the western end of the fell generally known as High Green Field Knott, itself at the northern end of the long Birks Fell ridge.

Date	Parking ★ ★ ★ ★ ★	Map Ref: △ 22

Ascent Start Time	Trig Time

Descent Start Time	Finish Time

Ascent Duration	Descent Duration	Total Time

Total Distance Covered	No. Of Steps

Companions

Weather

Enjoyment ○ ○ ○ ○ ○ ○ ○ ○ ○ ○
Views ○ ○ ○ ○ ○ ○ ○ ○ ○ ○
Difficulty ○ ○ ○ ○ ○ ○ ○ ○ ○ ○

Highlights

Notes

Cow Close Fell

Height (m): 624m · Date Built: 8th September 1949 · County: North Yorkshire
Nearest Town: Barnoldswick · OS Grid Reference: SD884727
Cow Close Fell trig point is located on the summit of the hill above Littondale more commonly known as Darnbrook Fell.

Date	Parking ☆☆☆☆☆☆	Map Ref: /23\
Ascent Start Time		Trig Time
Descent Start Time		Finish Time
Ascent Duration	Descent Duration	Total Time
Total Distance Covered		No. Of Steps
Companions		

Weather

Enjoyment ○○○○○○○○○○

Views ○○○○○○○○○○

Difficulty ○○○○○○○○○○

Highlights

Notes

Crag Hill

Height (m): 683m · Date Built: 1st September 1949 · County: Cumbria
Nearest Town: Kendal · OS Grid Reference: SD692833

Crag Hill trig point is one of the finest viewpoints in the north-west Yorkshire Dales. The view of the Howgill Fells is magnificent. On a clear day the Irish Sea and the Lakeland Fells can also be seen in the distance.

Date	Parking ★ ★ ★ ★ ★	Map Ref: 24

Ascent Start Time	Trig Time

Descent Start Time	Finish Time

Ascent Duration	Descent Duration	Total Time

Total Distance Covered	No. Of Steps

Companions

Weather

Enjoyment ○ ○ ○ ○ ○ ○ ○ ○ ○ ○

Views ○ ○ ○ ○ ○ ○ ○ ○ ○ ○

Difficulty ○ ○ ○ ○ ○ ○ ○ ○ ○ ○

Highlights

Notes

Crook Rise Crag Top

Height (m): 415m · Date Built: 30th September 1949 · County: North Yorkshire
Nearest Town: Skipton · OS Grid Reference: SD987558

Crookrise Crag Top trig point is situated above an extensive gritstone crag on the western edge of Embsay Moor. It's a nice & fairly easy climb up to the trig point from the car park at Embsay Reservoir.

Date	Parking ★★★★★	Map Ref: /25\

Ascent Start Time	Trig Time

Descent Start Time	Finish Time

Ascent Duration	Descent Duration	Total Time

Total Distance Covered		No. Of Steps

Companions

Weather

Enjoyment ○ ○ ○ ○ ○ ○ ○ ○ ○ ○

Views ○ ○ ○ ○ ○ ○ ○ ○ ○ ○

Difficulty ○ ○ ○ ○ ○ ○ ○ ○ ○ ○

Highlights

Notes

Delph Farm

Height (m): 276m · Date Built: 23rd March 1949 · County: West Yorkshire
Nearest Town: Skipton · OS Grid Reference: SE017478

Delph Farm trig point is located in a field alongside Jackson's Lane, a minor road between Low Bradley and Silsden. It can be easily seen from the road, and access can be granted if you ask the 'Delph Feline Cattery' nicely!

Date	Parking ★ ★ ★ ★ ★	Map Ref: /26\
Ascent Start Time		Trig Time
Descent Start Time		Finish Time
Ascent Duration	Descent Duration	Total Time
Total Distance Covered		No. Of Steps
Companions		

Weather

Enjoyment ◯ ◯ ◯ ◯ ◯ ◯ ◯ ◯ ◯ ◯
Views ◯ ◯ ◯ ◯ ◯ ◯ ◯ ◯ ◯ ◯
Difficulty ◯ ◯ ◯ ◯ ◯ ◯ ◯ ◯ ◯ ◯

Highlights

Notes

Dodd Fell

Height (m): 668m · Date Built: 30th September 1949 · County: North Yorkshire
Nearest Town: Richmond · OS Grid Reference: SD840845

One of the most central trigs in the national park, the views are extensive and includes many of the higher fells in the Dales. It can be reached by a short but steep climb from the Pennine Way to the west as it passes along the flanks of Dodd Fell on the track known as the West Cam Road.

Date	Parking ★★★★★	Map Ref: /27\
Ascent Start Time		Trig Time
Descent Start Time		Finish Time
Ascent Duration	Descent Duration	Total Time
Total Distance Covered		No. Of Steps
Companions		

Weather

Enjoyment ○○○○○○○○○○
Views ○○○○○○○○○○
Difficulty ○○○○○○○○○○

Highlights

Notes

East Baugh Fell

Height (m): 676m · Date Built: 1st September 1949 · County: Cumbria
Nearest Town: Kendal · OS Grid Reference: SD731919
The trig point is 2m lower than the summit of Baugh Fell which is located two thirds of a mile away on Tarn Rigg Hill. The trig point is
listed as East Baugh Fell even though it is on the westernmost of Baugh Fell's two summits.

Date	Parking ★★★★★	Map Ref: 28

Ascent Start Time		Trig Time	

Descent Start Time		Finish Time	

Ascent Duration	Descent Duration	Total Time

Total Distance Covered	No. Of Steps

Companions

Weather

Enjoyment ◯◯◯◯◯◯◯◯◯◯

Views ◯◯◯◯◯◯◯◯◯◯

Difficulty ◯◯◯◯◯◯◯◯◯◯

Highlights

Notes

Firth Fell

Height (m): 607m · Date Built: 10th July 1949 · County: North Yorkshire
Nearest Town: Skipton · OS Grid Reference: SD925748

Firth Fell trig point is one of four trig points on the long Birks Fell ridge dividing Littondale and Wharfedale. The fell is generally known as Birks Fell, the highest point of which is a mile to the north on the other side of Birks Tarn.

Date	Parking ★★★★★	Map Ref: /29\
Ascent Start Time		Trig Time
Descent Start Time		Finish Time
Ascent Duration	Descent Duration	Total Time
Total Distance Covered		No. Of Steps
Companions		

Weather

Enjoyment ○○○○○○○○○○
Views ○○○○○○○○○○
Difficulty ○○○○○○○○○○

Highlights

Notes

Gragareth Fell

Height (m): 627m · Date Built: 1st May 1949 · County: Lancashire
Nearest Town: Carnforth · OS Grid Reference: SD687793

Gragareth Fell trig point is on the Lancashire side of the county boundary that runs along the top of the fell. The trig point does not quite stand at the highest point of Gragareth, a slightly higher point 100m east of the trig point meant Gragareth replaced neighbouring Green Hill as the county top of Lancashire in 2014.

Date	Parking ★ ★ ★ ★ ★	Map Ref: /30\
Ascent Start Time	Trig Time	
Descent Start Time	Finish Time	

Ascent Duration	Descent Duration	Total Time

Total Distance Covered	No. Of Steps

Companions

Weather

Enjoyment	○ ○ ○ ○ ○ ○ ○ ○ ○ ○
Views	○ ○ ○ ○ ○ ○ ○ ○ ○ ○
Difficulty	○ ○ ○ ○ ○ ○ ○ ○ ○ ○

Highlights

Notes

Great Knoutberry Hill

Height (m): 672m • Date Built: 23rd April 1955 • County: Cumbria
Nearest Town: Kendal • OS Grid Reference: SD788871

The panorama from the Great Knoutberry Hill trig point is excellent and includes all of the major hills of the western Dales. On a clear day the Lake District fells, including the Scafells and Great Gable can be seen.

Date	Parking ★★★★★	Map Ref: /31\

Ascent Start Time	Trig Time

Descent Start Time	Finish Time

Ascent Duration	Descent Duration	Total Time

Total Distance Covered	No. Of Steps

Companions

Weather

Enjoyment ○○○○○○○○○○

Views ○○○○○○○○○○

Difficulty ○○○○○○○○○○

Highlights

Notes

Great Shunner Fell

Height (m): 716m · Date Built: 14th October 1953 · County: North Yorkshire
Nearest Town: Richmond · OS Grid Reference: SD848972
Great Shunner Fell trig point is the third highest trig point in the Yorkshire Dales and is easy to miss as it is built into the summit wind shelter.

Date	Parking ★★★★★	Map Ref: /32\

Ascent Start Time	Trig Time

Descent Start Time	Finish Time

Ascent Duration	Descent Duration	Total Time

Total Distance Covered	No. Of Steps

Companions

Weather

Enjoyment ○○○○○○○○○○
Views ○○○○○○○○○○
Difficulty ○○○○○○○○○○

Highlights

Notes

Great Whernside

Height (m): 704m · Date Built: 1936 · County: North Yorkshire
Nearest Town: Skipton · OS Grid Reference: SE002739

Great Whernside trig point is the fifth highest trig point in the Yorkshire Dales and one of the earliest to be built, in 1936. The trig point is rather dominated by the large summit cairn just a few metres away.

Date	Parking ⭐⭐⭐⭐⭐	Map Ref: 33

Ascent Start Time		Trig Time
Descent Start Time		Finish Time
Ascent Duration	Descent Duration	Total Time
Total Distance Covered		No. Of Steps
Companions		

Weather

Enjoyment	○ ○ ○ ○ ○ ○ ○ ○ ○ ○
Views	○ ○ ○ ○ ○ ○ ○ ○ ○ ○
Difficulty	○ ○ ○ ○ ○ ○ ○ ○ ○ ○

Highlights

Notes

Green Bell

Height (m): 605m · Date Built: 29th May 1960 · County: cumbria
Nearest Town: Kendal · OS Grid Reference: NY698010

Green Bell trig point is on the hill of the same name in the Howgill Fells. All the summits in the Howgill Fells are superb for views and the panorama from the Green Bell trig point is one of the best on a fine, sunny day.

Date	Parking ★ ★ ★ ★ ★	Map Ref: /34\

Ascent Start Time		Trig Time	

Descent Start Time		Finish Time	

Ascent Duration	Descent Duration	Total Time

Total Distance Covered		No. Of Steps

Companions

Weather

Enjoyment	◯ ◯ ◯ ◯ ◯ ◯ ◯ ◯ ◯ ◯
Views	◯ ◯ ◯ ◯ ◯ ◯ ◯ ◯ ◯ ◯
Difficulty	◯ ◯ ◯ ◯ ◯ ◯ ◯ ◯ ◯ ◯

Highlights

Notes

Greenhow Moor

Height (m): 427m · Date Built: 27th October 1953 · County: North Yorkshire
Nearest Town: Ilkley · OS Grid Reference: SE124640

The Greenhow Moor trig point was built in 1953 but was destroyed when it fell victim to the expanding Coldstones Quarry near Greenhow in 1972. Access is now impossible, but worth a look around the surrounding area.

Date	Parking ⭐⭐⭐⭐⭐	Map Ref: /35\

Ascent Start Time		Trig Time	
Descent Start Time		Finish Time	

Ascent Duration	Descent Duration	Total Time

Total Distance Covered	No. Of Steps

Companions

Weather

Enjoyment	○○○○○○○○○○
Views	○○○○○○○○○○
Difficulty	○○○○○○○○○○

Highlights

Notes

Grey Grit

Height (m): 522m · Date Built: 1st April 1960 · County: Cumbria
Nearest Town: Appleby-In-Westmorland · OS Grid Reference: NY876088

Grey Grit trig point is on the summit of High Greygrits, a little known top two miles north-west of the Tan Hill Inn, located to the east of a disused quarry and features an extensive view of where the Yorkshire Dales merge into the North Pennines.

Date	Parking ★ ★ ★ ★ ★	Map Ref: /36\

Ascent Start Time		Trig Time	
Descent Start Time		Finish Time	

Ascent Duration	Descent Duration	Total Time

Total Distance Covered	No. Of Steps

Companions

Weather

Enjoyment	○ ○ ○ ○ ○ ○ ○ ○ ○ ○
Views	○ ○ ○ ○ ○ ○ ○ ○ ○ ○
Difficulty	○ ○ ○ ○ ○ ○ ○ ○ ○ ○

Highlights

Notes

Halton Height

Height (m): 357m · Date Built: 15th April 1949 · County: North Yorkshire
Nearest Town: Skipton · OS Grid Reference: SE030552
Situated between the village of Halton East and Lower Barden Reservoir, Halton Height trig point is situated on Halton Height, also known as High Crag.

Date	Parking ★★★★★	Map Ref: 37

Ascent Start Time	Trig Time
Descent Start Time	Finish Time

Ascent Duration	Descent Duration	Total Time

Total Distance Covered	No. Of Steps

Companions

Weather

Enjoyment ○○○○○○○○○○
Views ○○○○○○○○○○
Difficulty ○○○○○○○○○○

Highlights

Notes

Harper Hill

Height (m): 257m • Date Built: 26th October 1953 • County: North Yorkshire
Nearest Town: Ripon • OS Grid Reference: SE205700
Harper Hill trig point is situated in a small wood to the north of Skell Gill in the Nidderdale Area Of Outstanding Natural Beauty.

Date	Parking ★ ★ ★ ★ ★	Map Ref: △38

Ascent Start Time		Trig Time	
Descent Start Time		Finish Time	

Ascent Duration	Descent Duration	Total Time

Total Distance Covered	No. Of Steps

Companions

Weather

Enjoyment ○ ○ ○ ○ ○ ○ ○ ○ ○ ○

Views ○ ○ ○ ○ ○ ○ ○ ○ ○ ○

Difficulty ○ ○ ○ ○ ○ ○ ○ ○ ○ ○

Highlights

Notes

Hartwith

Height (m): 191m · Date Built: 29th March 1954 · County: North Yorkshire
Nearest Town: Harrogate · OS Grid Reference: SE210610

Hartwith trig point is located on a small hill in Nidderdale above the village of Darley. It is not in the best condition, showing signs of deterioration from years of harsh winters.

Date	Parking ★★★★★	Map Ref: △39

Ascent Start Time	Trig Time

Descent Start Time	Finish Time

Ascent Duration	Descent Duration	Total Time

Total Distance Covered	No. Of Steps

Companions

Weather

Enjoyment ◯◯◯◯◯◯◯◯◯◯

Views ◯◯◯◯◯◯◯◯◯◯

Difficulty ◯◯◯◯◯◯◯◯◯◯

Highlights

Notes

Haw Crag

Height (m): 207m · Date Built: 1st April 1949 · County: North Yorkshire
Nearest Town: Earby · OS Grid Reference: SD913564
Haw Crag trig point is located to the north-west of Gargrave and situated 300ft outside the boundary of the Yorkshire Dales National Park.

Date	Parking ★★★★★	Map Ref: ◣40

Ascent Start Time	Trig Time

Descent Start Time	Finish Time

Ascent Duration	Descent Duration	Total Time

Total Distance Covered	No. Of Steps

Companions

Weather

Enjoyment ○○○○○○○○○○

Views ○○○○○○○○○○

Difficulty ○○○○○○○○○○

Highlights

Notes

Haw Pike

Height (m): 253m · Date Built: 22nd April 1949 · County: North Yorkshire
Nearest Town: Ilkley · OS Grid Reference: SE059522

Haw Pike trig point is situated on the top of a small hill above Chelker Reservoir to the south west of the village of Bolton Abbey.

Date	Parking ★★★★★★★	Map Ref: /41\
Ascent Start Time		Trig Time
Descent Start Time		Finish Time
Ascent Duration	Descent Duration	Total Time
Total Distance Covered		No. Of Steps
Companions		

Weather

Enjoyment	○	○	○	○	○	○	○	○	○	○
Views	○	○	○	○	○	○	○	○	○	○
Difficulty	○	○	○	○	○	○	○	○	○	○

Highlights

Notes

Heyshaw Moor

Height (m): 332m · Date Built: 2nd November 1953 · County: North Yorkshire
Nearest Town: Harrogate · OS Grid Reference: SE165628

Heyshaw Moor trig point is on a small boulder on High Crag, with views of sprawling moorland and high pastures on Heyshaw Moor.

Date	Parking ★ ★ ★ ★ ★	Map Ref: 42

Ascent Start Time	Trig Time

Descent Start Time	Finish Time

Ascent Duration	Descent Duration	Total Time

Total Distance Covered	No. Of Steps

Companions

Weather

Enjoyment ○ ○ ○ ○ ○ ○ ○ ○ ○ ○
Views ○ ○ ○ ○ ○ ○ ○ ○ ○ ○
Difficulty ○ ○ ○ ○ ○ ○ ○ ○ ○ ○

Highlights

Notes

High Seat

Height (m): 709m · Date Built: Not known · County: North Yorkshire
Nearest Town: Appleby-In-Westmorland · OS Grid Reference: NY802012
High Seat trig point is situated close to the highest of three cairns found on the top of High Seat – with some fantastic views of the surrounding landscape.

Date	Parking ⭐⭐⭐⭐⭐	Map Ref: 43

Ascent Start Time	Trig Time

Descent Start Time	Finish Time

Ascent Duration	Descent Duration	Total Time

Total Distance Covered	No. Of Steps

Companions

Weather

Enjoyment	○	○	○	○	○	○	○	○	○	○
Views	○	○	○	○	○	○	○	○	○	○
Difficulty	○	○	○	○	○	○	○	○	○	○

Highlights

Notes

Holme Knott

Height (m): 350m • Date Built: 1st June 1949 • County: Cumbria
Nearest Town: Kendal • OS Grid Reference: SD646895
Holme Knott trig point is situated at the northern end of Middleton Fell, with views to the north of Sedbergh backed by the Howgill Fells.

Date	Parking ★ ★ ★ ★ ★	Map Ref: △ 44

Ascent Start Time		Trig Time	
Descent Start Time		Finish Time	

Ascent Duration	Descent Duration	Total Time

Total Distance Covered	No. Of Steps

Companions

Weather

Enjoyment	○ ○ ○ ○ ○ ○ ○ ○ ○ ○
Views	○ ○ ○ ○ ○ ○ ○ ○ ○ ○
Difficulty	○ ○ ○ ○ ○ ○ ○ ○ ○ ○

Highlights

Notes

Hoove Faggergill

Height (m): 554m · Date Built: 15th April 1948 · County: North Yorkshire
Nearest Town: Richmond · OS Grid Reference: NZ004073

The Hoove Faggergill trig point is located near the summit of Hoove, a moorland top above Arkengarthdale. It is not quite the highest point of the fell, which lies about 480m to the south-west (approximately 1.4m higher than the trig point).

Date	Parking ★★★★★★	Map Ref: 45

Ascent Start Time		Trig Time	
Descent Start Time		Finish Time	
Ascent Duration	Descent Duration		Total Time
Total Distance Covered		No. Of Steps	
Companions			

Weather

Enjoyment ○○○○○○○○○○
Views ○○○○○○○○○○
Difficulty ○○○○○○○○○○

Highlights

Notes

45

Horse Head

Height (m): 605m · Date Built: 6th July 1949 · County: North Yorkshire
Nearest Town: Richmond · OS Grid Reference: SD887779

Horse Head trig point is on Horse Head Moor and is one of four trig points on the long Birks Fell ridge. The trig point does not sit on the highest part of Horse Head, the summit itself is almost a mile away to the south-east.

Date	Parking ★ ★ ★ ★ ★	Map Ref: /46\

Ascent Start Time		Trig Time	
Descent Start Time		Finish Time	

Ascent Duration	Descent Duration	Total Time

Total Distance Covered	No. Of Steps

Companions

Weather

Enjoyment	○ ○ ○ ○ ○ ○ ○ ○ ○ ○
Views	○ ○ ○ ○ ○ ○ ○ ○ ○ ○
Difficulty	○ ○ ○ ○ ○ ○ ○ ○ ○ ○

Highlights

Notes

Hunter Bark

Height (m): 315m · Date Built: 26th June 1949 · County: North Yorkshire
Nearest Town: Barnoldswick · OS Grid Reference: SD826610
Situated on a modest hill of the same name between Settle and Long Preston, Hunter Bark trig point boasts fine views north up Ribblesdale towards Three Peaks country.

Date	Parking ★★★★★	Map Ref: /47\

Ascent Start Time	Trig Time

Descent Start Time	Finish Time

Ascent Duration	Descent Duration	Total Time

Total Distance Covered	No. Of Steps

Companions

Weather

Enjoyment ○○○○○○○○○○
Views ○○○○○○○○○○
Difficulty ○○○○○○○○○○

Highlights

Notes

Ingleborough

Height (m): 724m · Date Built: 30th August 1949 · County: North Yorkshire
Nearest Town: Carnforth · OS Grid Reference: SD741745

The Ingleborough trig point is made of stone, unlike most trig points in the Yorkshire Dales which are made of concrete. The views at 723m are extensive but due to the broad nature of the plateau lacks a bit of depth.

Date	Parking ★ ★ ★ ★ ★	Map Ref: /48\

Ascent Start Time	Trig Time

Descent Start Time	Finish Time

Ascent Duration	Descent Duration	Total Time

Total Distance Covered	No. Of Steps

Companions

Weather

Enjoyment ◯ ◯ ◯ ◯ ◯ ◯ ◯ ◯ ◯ ◯
Views ◯ ◯ ◯ ◯ ◯ ◯ ◯ ◯ ◯ ◯
Difficulty ◯ ◯ ◯ ◯ ◯ ◯ ◯ ◯ ◯ ◯

Highlights

Notes

Kelleth Rigg

Height (m): 307m · Date Built: 27th May 1960 · County: Cumbria
Nearest Town: Appleby-In-Westmorland · OS Grid Reference: NY663056

Situated above the tiny village of Kelleth in the upper Lune valley, the Kelleth Rigg trig point was originally north of the boundary of the Yorkshire Dales National Park, but was incorporated into the national park when the Orton Fells was extended in 2016.

Date	Parking ★★★★★★	Map Ref: 49

Ascent Start Time	Trig Time

Descent Start Time	Finish Time

Ascent Duration	Descent Duration	Total Time

Total Distance Covered	No. Of Steps

Companions

Weather

Enjoyment ○ ○ ○ ○ ○ ○ ○ ○ ○ ○
Views ○ ○ ○ ○ ○ ○ ○ ○ ○ ○
Difficulty ○ ○ ○ ○ ○ ○ ○ ○ ○ ○

Highlights

Notes

Kettlestang Hill

Height (m): 390m · Date Built: 24th October 1953 · County: North Yorkshire
Nearest Town: Ripon · OS Grid Reference: SE158711
Located near the Kettlestang Shooting House on Dallowgill Moor in the Nidderdale Area of Outstanding Natural Beauty – The trig point
is nestled in heathery moor with views of sweeping moorland.

Date	Parking ⭐⭐⭐⭐⭐	Map Ref: △50

Ascent Start Time	Trig Time

Descent Start Time	Finish Time

Ascent Duration	Descent Duration	Total Time

Total Distance Covered	No. Of Steps

Companions

Weather

Enjoyment ○○○○○○○○○○
Views ○○○○○○○○○○
Difficulty ○○○○○○○○○○

Highlights

Notes

Kex Gill Moor

Height (m): 303m · Date Built: Not known · County: North Yorkshire
Nearest Town: Harrogate · OS Grid Reference: SE143558

Kex Gill Moor trig point is one of a number of trig points in the country that has become the victim of quarrying. There is now a quarry pool where the trig point used to be located, but the site is worth a visit just to tick it off the list!

Date	Parking ⭐⭐⭐⭐⭐	Map Ref: 51

Ascent Start Time	Trig Time

Descent Start Time	Finish Time

Ascent Duration	Descent Duration	Total Time

Total Distance Covered	No. Of Steps

Companions

Weather

Enjoyment	◯ ◯ ◯ ◯ ◯ ◯ ◯ ◯ ◯ ◯
Views	◯ ◯ ◯ ◯ ◯ ◯ ◯ ◯ ◯ ◯
Difficulty	◯ ◯ ◯ ◯ ◯ ◯ ◯ ◯ ◯ ◯

Highlights

Notes

Kilnsey Moor

Height (m): 450m · Date Built: 26th June 1949 · County: North Yorkshire
Nearest Town: Skipton · OS Grid Reference: SD951660

Kilnsey Moor trig point is situated on a grassy hill above Mastiles Lane called Holgates Kilnsey Moor. The panoramas are good, particularly with Kilnsey Crag, Great Whernside and Buckden Pike all in view.

Date	Parking ★★★★★	Map Ref: /52\

Ascent Start Time	Trig Time

Descent Start Time	Finish Time

Ascent Duration	Descent Duration	Total Time

Total Distance Covered	No. Of Steps

Companions

Weather

Enjoyment ◯◯◯◯◯◯◯◯◯◯

Views ◯◯◯◯◯◯◯◯◯◯

Difficulty ◯◯◯◯◯◯◯◯◯◯

Highlights

Notes

Knowe Fell

Height (m): 593m · Date Built: 18th August 1949 · County: North Yorkshire
Nearest Town: Barnoldswick · OS Grid Reference: SD866685

Knowe Fell trig point is situated to the north-west of Malham Tarn and on a fine day it is one of the best trig points for views of Three Peaks country.

Date	Parking ★★★★★	Map Ref: /53\

Ascent Start Time		Trig Time
Descent Start Time		Finish Time

Ascent Duration	Descent Duration	Total Time

Total Distance Covered	No. Of Steps

Companions

Weather

Enjoyment ○○○○○○○○○○
Views ○○○○○○○○○○
Difficulty ○○○○○○○○○○

Highlights

Notes

Langcliffe

Height (m): 440m · Date Built: 30th July 1949 · County: North Yorkshire
Nearest Town: Barnoldswick · OS Grid Reference: SD833642
Langcliffe trig point is situated on Warrendale Knotts above Settle and Langcliffe. The views are good but are even better from the cairn at the northern end of the summit.

Date	Parking ★ ★ ★ ★ ★	Map Ref: /54\
Ascent Start Time		Trig Time
Descent Start Time		Finish Time
Ascent Duration	Descent Duration	Total Time
Total Distance Covered		No. Of Steps
Companions		

Weather

Enjoyment	○ ○ ○ ○ ○ ○ ○ ○ ○ ○
Views	○ ○ ○ ○ ○ ○ ○ ○ ○ ○
Difficulty	○ ○ ○ ○ ○ ○ ○ ○ ○ ○

Highlights

Notes

Langerton Hill

Height (m): 278m · Date Built: 13th May 1949 · County: North Yorkshire
Nearest Town: Skipton · OS Grid Reference: SE041622

Situated on a moderate hill north-east of Burnsall, the views are mainly of grassy landscapes with Thorpe Fell and Simon's Seat visible from the trig.

Date	Parking ★★★★★	Map Ref: 55

Ascent Start Time	Trig Time

Descent Start Time	Finish Time

Ascent Duration	Descent Duration	Total Time

Total Distance Covered	No. Of Steps

Companions

Weather

Enjoyment ○○○○○○○○○○

Views ○○○○○○○○○○

Difficulty ○○○○○○○○○○

Highlights

Notes

Lanshaw Farm

Height (m): 246m · Date Built: 9th November 1953 · County: North Yorkshire
Nearest Town: Otley · OS Grid Reference: SE241517

Lanshaw Farm trig point is easy to reach, a mere 5-10 minutes walk from the car park of Norwood Lane. The trig point is just on the other side of a low wall from the path.

Date	Parking ★ ★ ★ ★ ★	Map Ref: /56\

Ascent Start Time		Trig Time	
Descent Start Time		Finish Time	

Ascent Duration	Descent Duration	Total Time

Total Distance Covered	No. Of Steps

Companions

Weather

Enjoyment	◯ ◯ ◯ ◯ ◯ ◯ ◯ ◯ ◯ ◯
Views	◯ ◯ ◯ ◯ ◯ ◯ ◯ ◯ ◯ ◯
Difficulty	◯ ◯ ◯ ◯ ◯ ◯ ◯ ◯ ◯ ◯

Highlights

Notes

Lindley Moor

Height (m): 291m • Date Built: 19th November 1953 • County: North Yorkshire
Nearest Town: Otley • OS Grid Reference: SE214513

Located on top of a large boulder on Norwood Edge, the Lindley Moor trig point can be out of reach unless you are an agile scrambler.
It is possible though, and views to the north and south can be rewarding if you manage it.

Date	Parking ★★★★★	Map Ref: 57

Ascent Start Time	Trig Time

Descent Start Time	Finish Time

Ascent Duration	Descent Duration	Total Time

Total Distance Covered	No. Of Steps

Companions

Weather

Enjoyment ○○○○○ ○○○○○

Views ○○○○○ ○○○○○

Difficulty ○○○○○ ○○○○○

Highlights

Notes

Ling Park

Height (m): 245m · Date Built: 30th April 1949 · County: North Yorkshire
Nearest Town: Ilkley · OS Grid Reference: SE106504
Located on a bend of the minor road running from Beamsley to Middleton, possibly the easiest trig point to reach as it is only a few
metres away from a parking area on the road bend.

Date	Parking ★ ★ ★ ★ ★	Map Ref: /58\

Ascent Start Time	Trig Time

Descent Start Time	Finish Time

Ascent Duration	Descent Duration	Total Time

Total Distance Covered	No. Of Steps

Companions

Weather

Enjoyment ○ ○ ○ ○ ○ ○ ○ ○ ○ ○
Views ○ ○ ○ ○ ○ ○ ○ ○ ○ ○
Difficulty ○ ○ ○ ○ ○ ○ ○ ○ ○ ○

Highlights

Notes

Little Whernside

Height (m): 736m · Date Built: Not known · County: North Yorkshire
Nearest Town: Carnforth · OS Grid Reference: SD738814
Little Whernside trig point is not actually on Little Whernside at all - but on the much higher Whernside (18 miles away). The views to the west are superb on clear days.

Date	Parking ★★★★★	Map Ref: /59\

Ascent Start Time		Trig Time
Descent Start Time		Finish Time

Ascent Duration	Descent Duration	Total Time

Total Distance Covered		No. Of Steps

Companions

Weather

Enjoyment ○○○○○○○○○○
Views ○○○○○○○○○○
Difficulty ○○○○○○○○○○

Highlights

Notes

Low Green Field Lings

Height (m): 501m · Date Built: 20th September 1949 · County: North Yorkshire
Nearest Town: Richmond · OS Grid Reference: SD838808

With a better than expected view of both Ingleborough and Whernside, the approach is rough and boggy. The trig point does not sit on the summit of the fell – its actually located approx. 500ft to the south west of the summit.

Date	Parking ★★★★★	Map Ref: /60\

Ascent Start Time	Trig Time

Descent Start Time	Finish Time

Ascent Duration	Descent Duration	Total Time

Total Distance Covered	No. Of Steps

Companions

Weather

Enjoyment ○○○○○○○○○○
Views ○○○○○○○○○○
Difficulty ○○○○○○○○○○

Highlights

Notes

Mark Hill

Height (m): 459m · Date Built: 18th April 1955 · County: North Yorkshire
Nearest Town: Ripon · OS Grid Reference: SE090690

Located on the moorland between Grimwith Reservoir and upper Nidderdale, in a remote location in grassy wilderness. The panaroma is good, on fine days you can see for miles.

Date	Parking ★★★★★★	Map Ref: /61\
Ascent Start Time		Trig Time
Descent Start Time		Finish Time
Ascent Duration	Descent Duration	Total Time
Total Distance Covered		No. Of Steps
Companions		

Weather

Enjoyment	○	○	○	○	○	○	○	○	○ ○
Views	○	○	○	○	○	○	○	○	○ ○
Difficulty	○	○	○	○	○	○	○	○	○ ○

Highlights

Notes

Maulds Meaburn Moor

Height (m): 293m · Date Built: 4th April 1960 · County: Cumbria
Nearest Town: Appleby-In-Westmorland · OS Grid Reference: NY638152
Situated on a field above the villages of Crosby Ravensworth and Maulds Meaburn, the Maulds Meaburn Moor trig point was
incorporated into the Yorkshire Dales National Park when the boundaries extended in 2016.

Date	Parking ★★★★★	Map Ref: 62

Ascent Start Time		Trig Time	
Descent Start Time		Finish Time	

Ascent Duration	Descent Duration	Total Time

Total Distance Covered	No. Of Steps

Companions

Weather

Enjoyment ○○○○○○○○○○
Views ○○○○○○○○○○
Difficulty ○○○○○○○○○○

Highlights

Notes

Meugher

Height (m): 575m · Date Built: 7th June 1950 · County: North Yorkshire
Nearest Town: Skipton · OS Grid Reference: SE044704

The Meugher trig point sits on the summit of a remote moorland top in the Nidderdale Area of Outstanding Natural Beauty, quite possibly the remotest in the Yorkshire dales.

Date	Parking ☆☆☆☆☆	Map Ref: /63\

Ascent Start Time		Trig Time	
Descent Start Time		Finish Time	

Ascent Duration	Descent Duration	Total Time

Total Distance Covered	No. Of Steps

Companions

Weather

Enjoyment	○ ○ ○ ○ ○ ○ ○ ○ ○ ○
Views	○ ○ ○ ○ ○ ○ ○ ○ ○ ○
Difficulty	○ ○ ○ ○ ○ ○ ○ ○ ○ ○

Highlights

Notes

Middleham Low Moor

Height (m): 236m · Date Built: 19th August 1953 · County: North Yorkshire
Nearest Town: Richmond · OS Grid Reference: SE105874

Situated on the moor of the same name close by to some gallops. The panorama is impressive considering the altitude, with good views of Wensleydale including Castle Bolton and Leyburn on fine days.

Date	Parking ★★★★★	Map Ref: △64

Ascent Start Time	Trig Time

Descent Start Time	Finish Time

Ascent Duration	Descent Duration	Total Time

Total Distance Covered	No. Of Steps

Companions

Weather

Enjoyment ○○○○○○○○○○

Views ○○○○○○○○○○

Difficulty ○○○○○○○○○○

Highlights

Notes

Middlesmoor Pasture

Height (m): 434m • Date Built: 20th September 1949 • County: North Yorkshire
Nearest Town: Skipton • OS Grid Reference: SD963710

Middlesmoor Pasture trig point is the most southerly of the four trig points on the long Birks Fell ridge between Littondale and Wharfedale, with magnificent views.

Date	Parking ☆☆☆☆☆	Map Ref: /65\

Ascent Start Time	Trig Time

Descent Start Time	Finish Time

Ascent Duration	Descent Duration	Total Time

Total Distance Covered	No. Of Steps

Companions

Weather

Enjoyment	○ ○ ○ ○ ○ ○ ○ ○ ○ ○
Views	○ ○ ○ ○ ○ ○ ○ ○ ○ ○
Difficulty	○ ○ ○ ○ ○ ○ ○ ○ ○ ○

Highlights

Notes

Middleton

Height (m): 486m · Date Built: 20th May 1960 · County: Cumbria
Nearest Town: kendal · OS Grid Reference: NY652012
Situated on Middleton, the long northern ridge of Simon's Seat in the Howgill Fells, it is the most northerly of only four trig points in the Howgill Fells.

Date	Parking ★ ★ ★ ★ ★	Map Ref: 66
Ascent Start Time		Trig Time
Descent Start Time		Finish Time
Ascent Duration	Descent Duration	Total Time
Total Distance Covered		No. Of Steps
Companions		

Weather

Enjoyment ○ ○ ○ ○ ○ ○ ○ ○ ○ ○
Views ○ ○ ○ ○ ○ ○ ○ ○ ○ ○
Difficulty ○ ○ ○ ○ ○ ○ ○ ○ ○ ○

Highlights

Notes

Moughton

Height (m): 428m · Date Built: 7th September 1949 · County: North Yorkshire
Nearest Town: Barnoldswick · OS Grid Reference: SD786711

The 360 degree view is excellent from the Moughton trig point, with fine views of Ingleborough and Pen-y-ghent. Also in view are Fountains Fell, Darnbrook Fell and to the south, Pendle Hill.

Date	Parking ★★★★★★	Map Ref: /67\

Ascent Start Time		Trig Time	
Descent Start Time		Finish Time	

Ascent Duration	Descent Duration	Total Time

Total Distance Covered	No. Of Steps

Companions

Weather

Enjoyment	○	○	○	○	○	○	○	○	○
Views	○	○	○	○	○	○	○	○	○
Difficulty	○	○	○	○	○	○	○	○	○

Highlights

Notes

Nettle Hill

Height (m): 382m · Date Built: 10th May 1960 · County: Cumbria
Nearest Town: Appleby-In-Westmorland · OS Grid Reference: NY716078
Situated on Crosby Garrett Fell in Westmoreland's Orton Fells, the Nettle Hill trig point is one of the youngest trig points in the Yorkshire Dales.

Date	Parking ★★★★★	Map Ref: /68\

Ascent Start Time	Trig Time

Descent Start Time	Finish Time

Ascent Duration	Descent Duration	Total Time

Total Distance Covered	No. Of Steps

Companions

Weather

Enjoyment ○○○○○○○○○○
Views ○○○○○○○○○○
Difficulty ○○○○○○○○○○

Highlights

Notes

New Pasture Edge

Height (m): 396m · Date Built: 20th August 1949 · County: North Yorkshire
Nearest Town: Skipton · OS Grid Reference: SE013663

New Pasture Edge trig point is situated on heather moorland near the former lead mines on Grassington Moor. The view includes Great Whernside, Simon's Seat and Cracoe Fell.

Date	Parking ☆☆☆☆☆	Map Ref: /69\

Ascent Start Time	Trig Time

Descent Start Time	Finish Time

Ascent Duration	Descent Duration	Total Time

Total Distance Covered		No. Of Steps

Companions

Weather

Enjoyment ○○○○○○○○○○

Views ○○○○○○○○○○

Difficulty ○○○○○○○○○○

Highlights

Notes

Newsham Moor

Height (m): 447m · Date Built: 10th November 1947 · County: Durham
Nearest Town: Barnard Castle · OS Grid Reference: NZ057074
Newsham Moor trig point is situated above Barningham Moor, a couple of miles outside the north-east boundary of the Yorkshire Dales National Park.

Date	Parking ★ ★ ★ ★ ★	Map Ref: /70

Ascent Start Time	Trig Time

Descent Start Time	Finish Time

Ascent Duration	Descent Duration	Total Time

Total Distance Covered	No. Of Steps

Companions

Weather

Enjoyment	○ ○ ○ ○ ○ ○ ○ ○ ○ ○
Views	○ ○ ○ ○ ○ ○ ○ ○ ○ ○
Difficulty	○ ○ ○ ○ ○ ○ ○ ○ ○ ○

Highlights

Notes

Newton Moor

Height (m): 292m · Date Built: 21st June 1949 · County: North Yorkshire
Nearest Town: Barnoldswick · OS Grid Reference: SD858587
Situated on the open access land of Newton Moor, views include Warrendale Knotts, Rye Loaf Hill, Kirkby Fell, Weets Top, Cracoe Fell, Sharp Haw and Ingleborough.

Date	Parking ★★★★★	Map Ref: /71\

Ascent Start Time	Trig Time

Descent Start Time	Finish Time

Ascent Duration	Descent Duration	Total Time

Total Distance Covered	No. Of Steps

Companions

Weather

Enjoyment ○○○○○○○○○○
Views ○○○○○○○○○○
Difficulty ○○○○○○○○○○

Highlights

Notes

Nine Standards Rigg

Height (m): 662m · Date Built: 20th May 1960 · County: Cumbria
Nearest Town: Appleby-In-Westmorland · OS Grid Reference: NY825061
The trig point is on a slight rise on the peaty summit of Nine Standards Rigg. It lies on the Coast to Coast route, and stands in the shadow of the nine standards themselves.

Date	Parking ★ ★ ★ ★ ★	Map Ref: /72\

Ascent Start Time		Trig Time	
Descent Start Time		Finish Time	

Ascent Duration	Descent Duration	Total Time

Total Distance Covered	No. Of Steps

Companions

Weather

Enjoyment	○	○	○	○	○	○	○	○	○	○
Views	○	○	○	○	○	○	○	○	○	○
Difficulty	○	○	○	○	○	○	○	○	○	○

Highlights

Notes

North Nab

Height (m): 319m · Date Built: 10th May 1949 · County: North Yorkshire
Nearest Town: Skipton · OS Grid Reference: SE084564

The North Nab trig point is on a spur of Hazelwood Moor overlooking Bolton Abbey and Strid Wood. A short walk to nearby South Nab and the great view down to the River Wharfe and Bolton Abbey is worth it.

Date	Parking ★★★★★	Map Ref: /73\

Ascent Start Time	Trig Time

Descent Start Time	Finish Time

Ascent Duration	Descent Duration	Total Time

Total Distance Covered	No. Of Steps

Companions

Weather

Enjoyment	○ ○ ○ ○ ○ ○ ○ ○ ○ ○
Views	○ ○ ○ ○ ○ ○ ○ ○ ○ ○
Difficulty	○ ○ ○ ○ ○ ○ ○ ○ ○ ○

Highlights

Notes

Ouster Bank

Height (m): 443m · Date Built: 11th September 1953 · County: North Yorkshire
Nearest Town: Ripon · OS Grid Reference: SE120751
Situated just south of the highest point of the Masham to Lofthouse road and offers views of moorland in all directions.

Date	Parking ★ ★ ★ ★ ★	Map Ref: /74\
Ascent Start Time		Trig Time
Descent Start Time		Finish Time
Ascent Duration	Descent Duration	Total Time
Total Distance Covered		No. Of Steps
Companions		

Weather

Enjoyment	○	○	○	○	○	○	○	○	○	○
Views	○	○	○	○	○	○	○	○	○	○
Difficulty	○	○	○	○	○	○	○	○	○	○

Highlights

Notes

Overgate Croft Farm

Height (m): 384m • Date Built: 23rd May 1949 • County: West Yorkshire
Nearest Town: Ilkley • OS Grid Reference: SE081466

The Overgate Croft Farm trig point is found on Addingham High Moor. While the views to the east is Ilkley Moor to the west there is a good view of Pendle Hill.

Date	Parking ★★★★★	Map Ref: /75\

Ascent Start Time	Trig Time
Descent Start Time	Finish Time

Ascent Duration	Descent Duration	Total Time

Total Distance Covered	No. Of Steps

Companions

Weather

Enjoyment	○ ○ ○ ○ ○ ○ ○ ○ ○ ○
Views	○ ○ ○ ○ ○ ○ ○ ○ ○ ○
Difficulty	○ ○ ○ ○ ○ ○ ○ ○ ○ ○

Highlights

Notes

Park Fell

Height (m): 564m · Date Built: 14th August 1949 · County: North Yorkshire
Nearest Town: Carnforth · OS Grid Reference: SD764769

The Park Fell trig point is well placed for a fantastic panorama of upper Ribblesdale, including the valley and not just the surrounding fells of Pen-y-ghent, Plover Hill, High Green Field Knott, Blea Moor, Whernside and Simon Fell.

Date	Parking ★★★★★	Map Ref: /76\

Ascent Start Time	Trig Time

Descent Start Time	Finish Time

Ascent Duration	Descent Duration	Total Time

Total Distance Covered	No. Of Steps

Companions

Weather

Enjoyment ○○○○○○○○○○

Views ○○○○○○○○○○

Difficulty ○○○○○○○○○○

Highlights

Notes

Parsons Pulpit

Height (m): 538m · Date Built: Not known · County: North Yorkshire
Nearest Town: Skipton · OS Grid Reference: SD918687

The Parsons Pulpit trig point is listed as being destroyed in 1986 and replaced by a surface block. It is possible that the block there now is in fact the surviving base of the original trig point.

Date	Parking ★★★★★	Map Ref: /77\

Ascent Start Time		Trig Time	
Descent Start Time		Finish Time	

Ascent Duration	Descent Duration	Total Time

Total Distance Covered	No. Of Steps

Companions

Weather

Enjoyment	○○○○○○○○○○
Views	○○○○○○○○○○
Difficulty	○○○○○○○○○○

Highlights

Notes

Pen-Y-Ghent

Height (m): 695m · Date Built: 11th November 1949 · County: North Yorkshire
Nearest Town: Barnoldswick · OS Grid Reference: SD838733
Pen-Y-Ghent trig point is located on the summit Penyghent. A stone built trig point as opposed to the more commonly found concrete pillars – with excellent views on a fine day.

Date	Parking ★ ★ ★ ★ ★	Map Ref: /78\

Ascent Start Time		Trig Time	
Descent Start Time		Finish Time	

Ascent Duration	Descent Duration	Total Time

Total Distance Covered	No. Of Steps

Companions

Weather

Enjoyment	○ ○ ○ ○ ○ ○ ○ ○ ○ ○
Views	○ ○ ○ ○ ○ ○ ○ ○ ○ ○
Difficulty	○ ○ ○ ○ ○ ○ ○ ○ ○ ○

Highlights

Notes

Penhill

Height (m): 527m · Date Built: 26th August 1953 · County: North Yorkshire
Nearest Town: Richmond · OS Grid Reference: SE050867

The Penhill trig point is situated on the hill of the same name, situated on the south side of a broken down wall and fence. These obscure the view, so it is worth making the short detour north to the top of Penhill Scar.

Date	Parking ☆☆☆☆☆☆	Map Ref: /79\

Ascent Start Time	Trig Time

Descent Start Time	Finish Time

Ascent Duration	Descent Duration	Total Time

Total Distance Covered	No. Of Steps

Companions

Weather

Enjoyment ○○○○○○○○○○
Views ○○○○○○○○○○
Difficulty ○○○○○○○○○○

Highlights

Notes

Powson Knott

Height (m): 413m · Date Built: 5th May 1960 · County: Cumbria
Nearest Town: Appleby-In-Westmorland · OS Grid Reference: NY646092
Powson Knott trig point is situated on Great Asby Scar in Westmoreland's Orton Fells. On a clear day the view extends west to the Lake District with the outline of Blencathra identifiable.

Date	Parking ★ ★ ★ ★ ★	Map Ref: /80\

Ascent Start Time	Trig Time

Descent Start Time	Finish Time

Ascent Duration	Descent Duration	Total Time

Total Distance Covered	No. Of Steps

Companions

Weather

Enjoyment ○ ○ ○ ○ ○ ○ ○ ○ ○ ○

Views ○ ○ ○ ○ ○ ○ ○ ○ ○ ○

Difficulty ○ ○ ○ ○ ○ ○ ○ ○ ○ ○

Highlights

Notes

Rain Stang Hill

Height (m): 454m · Date Built: 8th September 1953 · County: North Yorkshire
Nearest Town: Richmond · OS Grid Reference: SE080757

The Rain Stang Hill trig point is situated on a subsidary top of Woodale Moss in upper Nidderdale. The view is dominated by moorland tops including Great Whernside, Little Whernside, Dead Man's Hill and Great Haw.

Date	Parking ★ ★ ★ ★ ★	Map Ref: 81

Ascent Start Time	Trig Time

Descent Start Time	Finish Time

Ascent Duration	Descent Duration	Total Time

Total Distance Covered	No. Of Steps

Companions

Weather

Enjoyment	○	○	○	○	○	○	○	○	○	○
Views	○	○	○	○	○	○	○	○	○	○
Difficulty	○	○	○	○	○	○	○	○	○	○

Highlights

Notes

Ravensworth Fell

Height (m): 401m · Date Built: 18th May 1960 · County: Cumbria
Nearest Town: Appleby-In-Westmorland · OS Grid Reference: NY593108
The Ravensworth Fell trig point is situated on Long Scar Pike, the highest point of Crosby Ravensworth Fell. The 360 degree panorama is superb and includes the Howgill Fells, Shap Fells, Far Eastern Fells, the Cross Fell range and the fells above Mallerstang.

Date	Parking ★★★★★	Map Ref: /82\

Ascent Start Time	Trig Time

Descent Start Time	Finish Time

Ascent Duration	Descent Duration	Total Time

Total Distance Covered	No. Of Steps

Companions

Weather

Enjoyment ○○○○○○○○○○

Views ○○○○○○○○○○

Difficulty ○○○○○○○○○○

Highlights

Notes

Rivock Edge

Height (m): 359m · Date Built: 1st May 1948 · County: West Yorkshire
Nearest Town: Keighley · OS Grid Reference: SE074444

Rivock Edge trig point is situated above a plantation on the south-west corner of Rombalds Moor – and it isn't situated on access land.
The views are limited due to surrounding trees and boulders.

Date	Parking ★★★★★	Map Ref: /83\
Ascent Start Time		Trig Time
Descent Start Time		Finish Time
Ascent Duration	Descent Duration	Total Time
Total Distance Covered		No. Of Steps
Companions		

Weather

Enjoyment	○	○	○	○	○	○	○	○	○	○
Views	○	○	○	○	○	○	○	○	○	○
Difficulty	○	○	○	○	○	○	○	○	○	○

Highlights

Notes

Rombalds Moor

Height (m): 403m · Date Built: 1936 · County: West Yorkshire
Nearest Town: Ilkley · OS Grid Reference: SE114452

The trig point is located on the highest part of Ilkley Moor, the views are extensive and on a clear day, from Wharfedale to Great Whernside and as far east as the Hambleton Hills with the Kilburn White Horse also visible in the distance.

Date	Parking ★★★★★	Map Ref: /84\

Ascent Start Time	Trig Time

Descent Start Time	Finish Time

Ascent Duration	Descent Duration	Total Time

Total Distance Covered	No. Of Steps

Companions

Weather

Enjoyment	◯ ◯ ◯ ◯ ◯ ◯ ◯ ◯ ◯ ◯
Views	◯ ◯ ◯ ◯ ◯ ◯ ◯ ◯ ◯ ◯
Difficulty	◯ ◯ ◯ ◯ ◯ ◯ ◯ ◯ ◯ ◯

Highlights

Notes

Rye Loaf

Height (m): 547m · Date Built: 10th August 1949 · County: North Yorkshire
Nearest Town: Barnoldswick · OS Grid Reference: SD864633
Situated on the summit of Rye Loaf Hill between Malham and Settle, the views are exceptional incorporating the Three Peaks but also an extensive view south that includes Pendle Hill and the Bowland Fells.

Date	Parking ★★★★★	Map Ref: /85\
Ascent Start Time		Trig Time
Descent Start Time		Finish Time
Ascent Duration	Descent Duration	Total Time
Total Distance Covered		No. Of Steps
Companions		

Weather

Enjoyment ○ ○ ○ ○ ○ ○ ○ ○ ○ ○
Views ○ ○ ○ ○ ○ ○ ○ ○ ○ ○
Difficulty ○ ○ ○ ○ ○ ○ ○ ○ ○ ○

Highlights

Notes

Sail Hill

Height (m): 259m · Date Built: 27th September 1953 · County: North Yorkshire
Nearest Town: Ripon · OS Grid Reference: SE172830
The Sail Hill trig point is situated near the village of Ellingstring in the north west of the Nidderdale Area of Outstanding Natural Beauty.

Date	Parking ⭐⭐⭐⭐⭐	Map Ref: /86\

Ascent Start Time	Trig Time
Descent Start Time	Finish Time

Ascent Duration	Descent Duration	Total Time

Total Distance Covered	No. Of Steps

Companions

Weather

Enjoyment	◯◯◯◯◯◯◯◯◯◯
Views	◯◯◯◯◯◯◯◯◯◯
Difficulty	◯◯◯◯◯◯◯◯◯◯

Highlights

Notes

Sandy Hill

Height (m): 359m · Date Built: 14th September 1953 · County: North Yorkshire
Nearest Town: Ripon · OS Grid Reference: SE165755

The Sandy Hill trig point is located on a rocky outcrop amongst a sea of heather on Masham Moor, with distant views of Great Whernside and Little Whernside visible on clear days.

Date	Parking ★★★★★★	Map Ref: /87\

Ascent Start Time		Trig Time
Descent Start Time		Finish Time

Ascent Duration	Descent Duration	Total Time

Total Distance Covered	No. Of Steps

Companions

Weather

Enjoyment ○○○○○○○○○○

Views ○○○○○○○○○○

Difficulty ○○○○○○○○○○

Highlights

Notes

Scrafton

Height (m): 472m · Date Built: Not known · County: North Yorkshire
Nearest Town: Richmond · OS Grid Reference: SE082824

Scrafton trig point is actually a bolt in one of the rocks of Great Roova Crags, with superb views of Coverdale, Pen Hill and the villages of Carlton, Melmerby and West Scrafton.

Date	Parking ★★★★★	Map Ref: △88
Ascent Start Time		Trig Time
Descent Start Time		Finish Time
Ascent Duration	Descent Duration	Total Time
Total Distance Covered		No. Of Steps
Companions		

Weather

Enjoyment ○○○○○○○○○○
Views ○○○○○○○○○○
Difficulty ○○○○○○○○○○

Highlights

Notes

Sharpah

Height (m): 357m · Date Built: 25th May 1949 · County: North Yorkshire
Nearest Town: Skipton · OS Grid Reference: SD959552

Sharpah trig point is located on the highest point of Flasby Fell, the summit of Sharp Haw. This one's also a Marilyn, so unsurprisingly the views of Airedale and the Aire Gap with Gargrave and Skipton are magnificent.

Date	Parking ⭐⭐⭐⭐⭐	Map Ref: /89\

Ascent Start Time	Trig Time

Descent Start Time	Finish Time

Ascent Duration	Descent Duration	Total Time

Total Distance Covered	No. Of Steps

Companions

Weather

Enjoyment ○ ○ ○ ○ ○ ○ ○ ○ ○ ○

Views ○ ○ ○ ○ ○ ○ ○ ○ ○ ○

Difficulty ○ ○ ○ ○ ○ ○ ○ ○ ○ ○

Highlights

Notes

Simons Seat

Height (m): 485m · Date Built: 1st April 1949 · County: North Yorkshire
Nearest Town: Skipton · OS Grid Reference: SE078598

Simons Seat trig point is located on the summit of the same name, with great views of gritstone moor and the surrounding mountains in the distance also visible on a clear day.

Date	Parking ★★★★★	Map Ref: /90\

Ascent Start Time	Trig Time

Descent Start Time	Finish Time

Ascent Duration	Descent Duration	Total Time

Total Distance Covered	No. Of Steps

Companions

Weather

Enjoyment	○ ○ ○ ○ ○ ○ ○ ○ ○ ○
Views	○ ○ ○ ○ ○ ○ ○ ○ ○ ○
Difficulty	○ ○ ○ ○ ○ ○ ○ ○ ○ ○

Highlights

Notes

Smearsett Scar

Height (m): 363m · Date Built: 24th July 1949 · County: North Yorkshire
Nearest Town: Barnoldswick · OS Grid Reference: SD802678
The views are excellent from the The Smearsett Scar trig point which includes Moughton as well as Ingleborough and Pen-y-ghent in the north Bowland fells.

Date	Parking ★★★★★★★	Map Ref: /91\

Ascent Start Time	Trig Time

Descent Start Time	Finish Time

Ascent Duration	Descent Duration	Total Time

Total Distance Covered	No. Of Steps

Companions

Weather

Enjoyment ○ ○ ○ ○ ○ ○ ○ ○ ○ ○

Views ○ ○ ○ ○ ○ ○ ○ ○ ○ ○

Difficulty ○ ○ ○ ○ ○ ○ ○ ○ ○ ○

Highlights

Notes

Stone Beds

Height (m): 232m · Date Built: 4th April 1955 · County: North Yorkshire
Nearest Town: Harrogate · OS Grid Reference: SE207579
The Stone Beds trig point is located in a field opposite RAF Menwith Hill, with a view which extends up the valley as far as Great Haw in the upper Nidderdale Area Of Outstanding Natural Beauty.

Date	Parking ★★★★★	Map Ref: /92\

Ascent Start Time	Trig Time

Descent Start Time	Finish Time

Ascent Duration	Descent Duration	Total Time

Total Distance Covered	No. Of Steps

Companions

Weather

Enjoyment ○○○○○○○○○○

Views ○○○○○○○○○○

Difficulty ○○○○○○○○○○

Highlights

Notes

Stonesdale Moor

Height (m): 549m · Date Built: Not known · County: North Yorkshire
Nearest Town: Barnard Castle · OS Grid Reference: NY871044

The Stonesdale Moor trig point is a concrete ring, a rare type of trig point mainly found in the Lake District and north-west Dales. It is fairly easy to reach with a short diversion from the path from Tan Hill to Ravenseat.

Date	Parking ★★★★★	Map Ref: /93\
Ascent Start Time		Trig Time
Descent Start Time		Finish Time
Ascent Duration	Descent Duration	Total Time
Total Distance Covered		No. Of Steps
Companions		

Weather

Enjoyment	○	○	○	○	○	○	○	○	○
Views	○	○	○	○	○	○	○	○	○
Difficulty	○	○	○	○	○	○	○	○	○

Highlights

Notes

Sulber

Height (m): 349m · Date Built: 12th July 1949 · County: North Yorkshire
Nearest Town: Barnoldswick · OS Grid Reference: SD787738
Sulber trig point is situated above a limestone scar to the north of Sulber Nick, with dominant views of Pen-y-ghent across the valley, Green Field Knott and Simon Fell.

Date	Parking ★★★★★	Map Ref: 94
Ascent Start Time		Trig Time
Descent Start Time		Finish Time
Ascent Duration	Descent Duration	Total Time
Total Distance Covered		No. Of Steps
Companions		
Weather		

Enjoyment ○○○○○○○○○○
Views ○○○○○○○○○○
Difficulty ○○○○○○○○○○

Highlights

Notes

Swinden

Height (m): 291m · Date Built: Not known · County: North Yorkshire
Nearest Town: Skipton · OS Grid Reference: SD976611

Swinden trig point was located on a small hill near the village of Cracoe, and has sadly become the victim of quarrying, thought to have been destroyed in 1990 as the Swinden Quarry expanded.

Date	Parking ⭐⭐⭐⭐⭐	Map Ref: /95\

| Ascent Start Time | | Trig Time | |
| Descent Start Time | | Finish Time | |

Ascent Duration	Descent Duration	Total Time

Total Distance Covered		No. Of Steps

Companions

Weather

Enjoyment ○ ○ ○ ○ ○ ○ ○ ○ ○ ○
Views   ○ ○ ○ ○ ○ ○ ○ ○ ○ ○
Difficulty ○ ○ ○ ○ ○ ○ ○ ○ ○ ○

Highlights

Notes

Telfit Moor

Height (m): 362m · Date Built: 1st February 1948 · County: North Yorkshire
Nearest Town: Richmond · OS Grid Reference: NZ077020

Telfit Moor trig point is above the valley of Marske Beck at the northern end of Skelton Moor. The views of the moors either side of the valley as well as the eastern side of Marrick Moor and Booze are wonderful on a fine day.

Date	Parking ★ ★ ★ ★ ★	Map Ref: 96

Ascent Start Time	Trig Time

Descent Start Time	Finish Time

Ascent Duration	Descent Duration	Total Time

Total Distance Covered	No. Of Steps

Companions

Weather

Enjoyment ○ ○ ○ ○ ○ ○ ○ ○ ○ ○

Views ○ ○ ○ ○ ○ ○ ○ ○ ○ ○

Difficulty ○ ○ ○ ○ ○ ○ ○ ○ ○ ○

Highlights

Notes

The Calf

Height (m): 677m · Date Built: 1st August 1949 · County: Cumbria
Nearest Town: Kendal · OS Grid Reference: SD667970

The Calf trig point is situated on the hill of the same name, the highest of the Howgill Fells. No surprise then that the view is superb across the Shap Fells to a long line of Lakeland summits.

Date	Parking ★★★★★	Map Ref: 97

Ascent Start Time	Trig Time

Descent Start Time	Finish Time

Ascent Duration	Descent Duration	Total Time

Total Distance Covered	No. Of Steps

Companions

Weather

Enjoyment ○ ○ ○ ○ ○ ○ ○ ○ ○ ○
Views   ○ ○ ○ ○ ○ ○ ○ ○ ○ ○
Difficulty ○ ○ ○ ○ ○ ○ ○ ○ ○ ○

Highlights

Notes

The Chevin

Height (m): 282m · Date Built: 6th July 1937 · County: West Yorkshire
Nearest Town: Otley · OS Grid Reference: SE199442

Originally built in 1937, the pillar is listed as having been destroyed in 1969. It presumably fell victim to Yorkgate Quarry which is now disused and used as a picnic area immediately below and to the west of the summit.

Date	Parking ★★★★★	Map Ref: /98\
Ascent Start Time		Trig Time
Descent Start Time		Finish Time
Ascent Duration	Descent Duration	Total Time
Total Distance Covered		No. Of Steps
Companions		

Weather

Enjoyment ○○○○○○○○○○
Views ○○○○○○○○○○
Difficulty ○○○○○○○○○○

Highlights

Notes

The Fleak

Height (m): 551m · Date Built: 1st May 1955 · County: North Yorkshire
Nearest Town: Richmond · OS Grid Reference: SD956943

The Fleak trig point is situated on a moorland top also known as Tarn Seat, a stone built trig point as opposed to one of the more common concrete versions. With extensive views, mainly of the moors above Wensleydale and Swaledale.

Date	Parking ★★★★★★	Map Ref: /99\

Ascent Start Time	Trig Time

Descent Start Time	Finish Time

Ascent Duration	Descent Duration	Total Time

Total Distance Covered	No. Of Steps

Companions

Weather

Enjoyment ○○○○○○○○○○
Views ○○○○○○○○○○
Difficulty ○○○○○○○○○○

Highlights

Notes

The Weets

Height (m): 414m · Date Built: 15th June 1949 · County: North Yorkshire
Nearest Town: Skipton · OS Grid Reference: SD925632
Weets trig point is located on Weets Top, a hill overlooking Malhamdale and Gordale.

Date	Parking ★★★★★	Map Ref: △100

Ascent Start Time	Trig Time

Descent Start Time	Finish Time

Ascent Duration	Descent Duration	Total Time

Total Distance Covered	No. Of Steps

Companions

Weather

Enjoyment	○○○○○○○○○○
Views	○○○○○○○○○○
Difficulty	○○○○○○○○○○

Highlights

Notes

Thorpe Fell

Height (m): 506m · Date Built: 18th May 1949 · County: North Yorkshire
Nearest Town: Skipton · OS Grid Reference: SE008596

Once reckoned the highest point of the moors between Embsay and and Cracoe, Thorpe Fell trig point lost this accolade following a survey in 2008, discovering that Cracoe Fell is slightly higher. As a result Thorpe Fell Top lost its status as a Dewey and a Marilyn.

Date	Parking ★★★★★	Map Ref: /101\

Ascent Start Time	Trig Time

Descent Start Time	Finish Time

Ascent Duration	Descent Duration	Total Time

Total Distance Covered	No. Of Steps

Companions

Weather

Enjoyment ○ ○ ○ ○ ○ ○ ○ ○ ○ ○

Views ○ ○ ○ ○ ○ ○ ○ ○ ○ ○

Difficulty ○ ○ ○ ○ ○ ○ ○ ○ ○ ○

Highlights

Notes

Tow Scar

Height (m): 383m · Date Built: 1st May 1949 · County: North Yorkshire
Nearest Town: Carnforth · OS Grid Reference: SD684760

Tow Scar trig point is located on a limestone scar at the southern end of Gragareth, and the view is particularly extensive looking south towards the northern Bowland Fells.

Date	Parking ★ ★ ★ ★ ★	Map Ref: △102
Ascent Start Time		Trig Time
Descent Start Time		Finish Time
Ascent Duration	Descent Duration	Total Time
Total Distance Covered		No. Of Steps
Companions		

Weather

Enjoyment	○ ○ ○ ○ ○ ○ ○ ○ ○ ○
Views	○ ○ ○ ○ ○ ○ ○ ○ ○ ○
Difficulty	○ ○ ○ ○ ○ ○ ○ ○ ○ ○

Highlights

Notes

Vicars Allotment

Height (m): 373m · Date Built: 28th May 1949 · County: North Yorkshire
Nearest Town: Skipton · OS Grid Reference: SE014509

Vicars Allotment trig point is located on the summit of Skipton Moor, with excellent views it is a mile and a half south of the national park boundary.

Date	Parking ⭑⭑⭑⭑⭑	Map Ref: /103\

Ascent Start Time		Trig Time
Descent Start Time		Finish Time
Ascent Duration	Descent Duration	Total Time
Total Distance Covered		No. Of Steps

Companions

Weather

Enjoyment ◯◯◯◯◯◯◯◯◯◯

Views ◯◯◯◯◯◯◯◯◯◯

Difficulty ◯◯◯◯◯◯◯◯◯◯

Highlights

Notes

Water Crag

Height (m): 668m · Date Built: 1936 · County: North Yorkshire
Nearest Town: Barnard Castle · OS Grid Reference: NY928046

One of the remoter trig points in the Yorkshire Dales, in good weather the view goes as far as the North York Moors in the east to the northern Lake District in the west. To the north-east you can see Little Fell and Mickle Fell.

Date	Parking ★ ★ ★ ★ ★	Map Ref: △104

Ascent Start Time	Trig Time

Descent Start Time	Finish Time

Ascent Duration	Descent Duration	Total Time

Total Distance Covered	No. Of Steps

Companions

Weather

Enjoyment ○ ○ ○ ○ ○ ○ ○ ○ ○ ○
Views ○ ○ ○ ○ ○ ○ ○ ○ ○ ○
Difficulty ○ ○ ○ ○ ○ ○ ○ ○ ○ ○

Highlights

Notes

Whaw Moor

Height (m): 584m · Date Built: 12th August 1948 · County: North Yorkshire
Nearest Town: Richmond · OS Grid Reference: NY970026

Whaw Moor trig point is located on the summit of the hill more commonly known as Great Pinseat. With good views north towards the high fells of the North Pennines including Mickle Fell and Little Fell.

Date	Parking ★★★★★	Map Ref: /105\

Ascent Start Time		Trig Time
Descent Start Time		Finish Time

Ascent Duration	Descent Duration	Total Time

Total Distance Covered		No. Of Steps

Companions

Weather

Enjoyment	○ ○ ○ ○ ○ ○ ○ ○ ○ ○
Views	○ ○ ○ ○ ○ ○ ○ ○ ○ ○
Difficulty	○ ○ ○ ○ ○ ○ ○ ○ ○ ○

Highlights

Notes

Whit Fell

Height (m): 412m · Date Built: 18th August 1953 · County: North Yorkshire
Nearest Town: Richmond · OS Grid Reference: SE086945

Whit Fell trig point is situated on top of the moor of the same name which is located within the MOD's Bellerby Range. Access is not advised without permission!

Date	Parking ★★★★★	Map Ref: △106

Ascent Start Time	Trig Time

Descent Start Time	Finish Time

Ascent Duration	Descent Duration	Total Time

Total Distance Covered	No. Of Steps

Companions

Weather

Enjoyment ○ ○ ○ ○ ○ ○ ○ ○ ○ ○

Views   ○ ○ ○ ○ ○ ○ ○ ○ ○ ○

Difficulty ○ ○ ○ ○ ○ ○ ○ ○ ○ ○

Highlights

Notes

Wild Boar Fell

Height (m): 709m · Date Built: 27th May 1960 · County: Cumbria
Nearest Town: Appleby-In-Westmorland · OS Grid Reference: SD757988

Wild Boar Fell trig point is located at the summit of Wild Boar Fell, surrounded by a stone shelter on the western side of the plateau. The views are quite spectacular including the Lakeland mountains, Howgill Fells and the old county of Westmorland.

Date	Parking ★★★★★★	Map Ref: /107\

Ascent Start Time	Trig Time

Descent Start Time	Finish Time

Ascent Duration	Descent Duration	Total Time

Total Distance Covered	No. Of Steps

Companions

Weather

Enjoyment	○	○	○	○	○	○	○	○	○	○
Views	○	○	○	○	○	○	○	○	○	○
Difficulty	○	○	○	○	○	○	○	○	○	○

Highlights

Notes

Winder Hill

Height (m): 474m · Date Built: 1st September 1949 · County: Cumbria
Nearest Town: Kendal · OS Grid Reference: SD653932

Situated on Winder, a hill at the southern end of the Howgill Fells, the Winder Hill trig point has a fantastic panorama including superb views of the Lune and Rawthey valleys as well as Garsdale and Dentdale.

Date	Parking ★ ★ ★ ★ ★	Map Ref: △108

Ascent Start Time	Trig Time

Descent Start Time	Finish Time

Ascent Duration	Descent Duration	Total Time

Total Distance Covered	No. Of Steps

Companions

Weather

Enjoyment ○ ○ ○ ○ ○ ○ ○ ○ ○ ○
Views ○ ○ ○ ○ ○ ○ ○ ○ ○ ○
Difficulty ○ ○ ○ ○ ○ ○ ○ ○ ○ ○

Highlights

Notes

Windy Hill

Height (m): 386m • Date Built: 27th May 1960 • County: Cumbria
Nearest Town: Appleby-In-Westmorland • OS Grid Reference: NY749040

Situated on Ash Fell in Westmorland's Orton Fells, not quite the highest point of the fell but the view still includes the Howgill Fells, Wild Boar Fell, High Seat, Nateby Common and Nine Standards Rigg.

Date	Parking ★★★★★	Map Ref: /109\

Ascent Start Time	Trig Time

Descent Start Time	Finish Time

Ascent Duration	Descent Duration	Total Time

Total Distance Covered	No. Of Steps

Companions

Weather

Enjoyment ○ ○ ○ ○ ○ ○ ○ ○ ○ ○

Views ○ ○ ○ ○ ○ ○ ○ ○ ○ ○

Difficulty ○ ○ ○ ○ ○ ○ ○ ○ ○ ○

Highlights

Notes

Witton Fell

Height (m): 351m · Date Built: 18th August 1953 · County: North Yorkshire
Nearest Town: Richmond · OS Grid Reference: SE132850

Witton Fell trig point is situated on a patch of moorland next to a conifer plantation on Witton Fell and is the easternmost trig point within the boundary of the Yorkshire Dales National Park.

Date	Parking ★★★★★	Map Ref: /110\

Ascent Start Time	Trig Time

Descent Start Time	Finish Time

Ascent Duration	Descent Duration	Total Time

Total Distance Covered	No. Of Steps

Companions

Weather

Enjoyment	○	○	○	○	○	○	○	○	○	○
Views	○	○	○	○	○	○	○	○	○	○
Difficulty	○	○	○	○	○	○	○	○	○	○

Highlights

Notes

Yockenthwaite Moor

Height (m): 643m · Date Built: 3rd August 1949 · County: North Yorkshire
Nearest Town: Richmond · OS Grid Reference: SD909810

Located on the summit of Yockenthwaite Moor, a fairly central location in the Dales with extensive views - The Three Peaks, Fountains Fell, Birks Fell, Buckden Pike – even the Coniston fells in the Lake District can be seen on a clear day.

Date	Parking	Map Ref: 111
Ascent Start Time	Trig Time	
Descent Start Time	Finish Time	
Ascent Duration	Descent Duration	Total Time
Total Distance Covered	No. Of Steps	
Companions		

Weather

Enjoyment ○ ○ ○ ○ ○ ○ ○ ○ ○ ○

Views ○ ○ ○ ○ ○ ○ ○ ○ ○ ○

Difficulty ○ ○ ○ ○ ○ ○ ○ ○ ○ ○

Highlights

Notes

Ready for your next adventure?

Keeping a log book is a fantastic way of recording your memories - and we have published a number of adventure log books available on Amazon. Simply scan the QR code to find out more!

Calling all hiking groups/businesses!

The next edition of this book will feature hiking/walking groups & businesses who organise trips or walks in the Dales. This is to offer our readers the opportunity to join these groups should they wish. To include your business or group is free of charge, so please contact us if you wish to be included. Spaces will be limited, please email us at *info@herbertpublishing.com* with your details.

NOTES / EMERGENCY CONTACTS

Printed in Great Britain
by Amazon

81295909R00072